Coral Polyps

Island
Inspirations

Photographs by Steve Simonsen

FRIENDS OF VIRGIN ISLANDS NATIONAL PARK
ST. JOHN, US VIRGIN ISLANDS

VIRGIN ISLANDS NATIONAL PARK
St. John, US Virgin Islands

Virgin Islands National Park is the Caribbean jewel of national parks. Defined by clear turquoise waters, white sand beaches, brightly colored coral reefs, and undeveloped rugged hillsides, St. John reflects a rich mix of cultural and natural history. Home to prehistoric relics, stone sugar mill ruins, and rare tropical species, Virgin Islands National Park tells the story of the Tainos and the petroglyphs, or "zemis," they left behind; of the Danish plantation era and slave revolt; and of the importance of biodiversity. The park has a network of trails highlighting its natural and cultural resources that affords visitors immersive interpretation and amazing views.

Thanks to the foresight and generous philanthropy of Laurance Rockefeller, the establishment of the Virgin Islands National Park has allowed locals and visitors alike to enjoy its trails and attractions, be inspired by its raw natural beauty, and seek respite from the stress of modern life. This scenic and historical treasure has been protected by the National Park Service since 1956.

May your trails be crooked, winding,
lonesome, dangerous, leading to the most
amazing view. May your mountains rise into
and above the clouds.

EDWARD ABBEY

Waterlemon Cay

Ocean: A body of water occupying about
two-thirds of a world made for man—
who has no gills.

AMBROSE BIERCE

Elkhorn Coral

The sea, once it casts its spell,
holds one in its net of wonder forever.

JACQUES-YVES COUSTEAU

I believe that there is a subtle magnetism
in Nature, which, if we unconsciously yield
to it, will direct us aright.

HENRY DAVID THOREAU

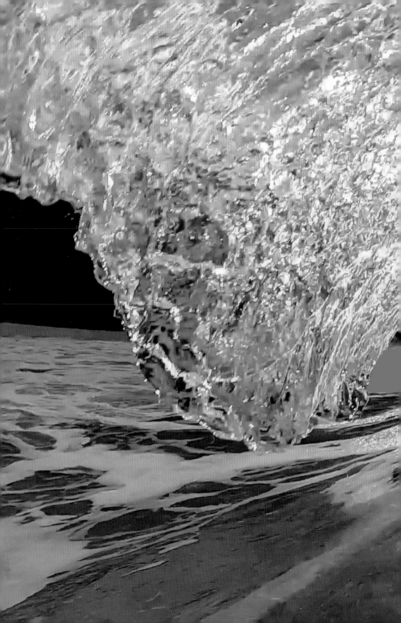

The boisterous sea of liberty is never without a wave.

Look deep into nature, and then you will understand everything better.

ALBERT EINSTEIN

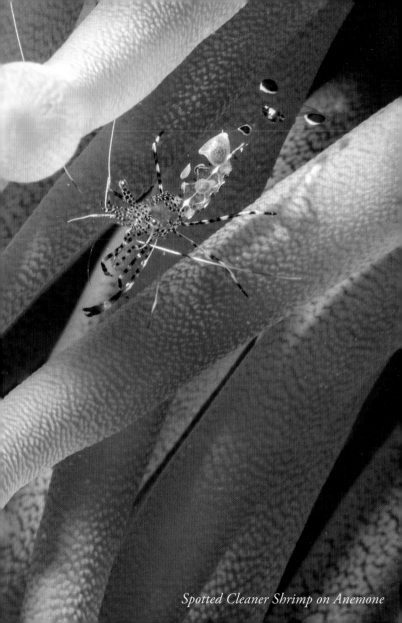

Spotted Cleaner Shrimp on Anemone

Banded Coral Shrimp

Caribbean Sharp-nose Puffer

There is nothing more enticing, disenchanting, and enslaving than the life at sea.

JOSEPH CONRAD

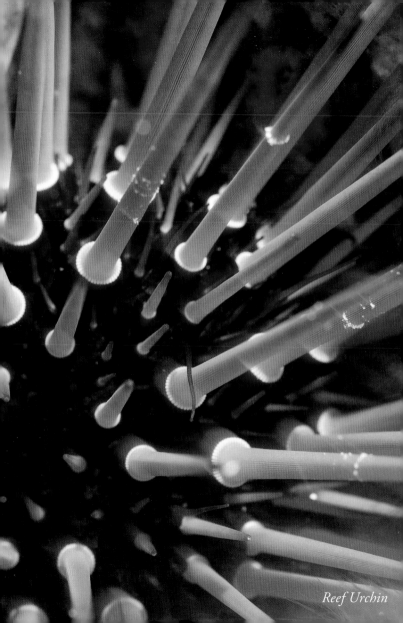

Reef Urchin

Warty Corallimorph

But to the eyes of the
man of imagination,
nature is imagination
itself.

WILLIAM BLAKE

Fingerprint Cyphoma

Flamingo Tongue

If you stand in one place long
enough, the world will come to you.

CHINESE PROVERB

Social Feather Dusters

Banded Tube-dwelling Anemone

There are no passengers on Spaceship
Earth. We are all crew.

MARSHALL MCLUHAN

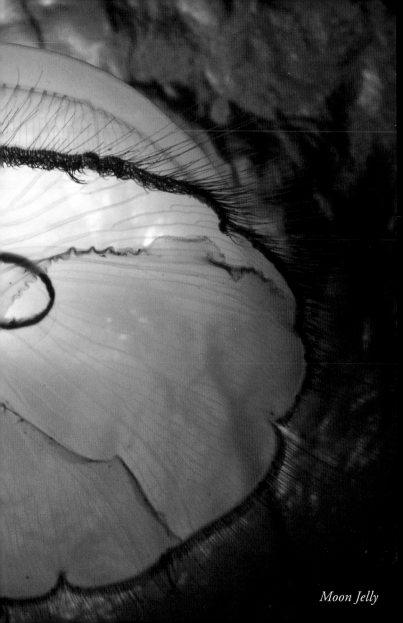

Moon Jelly

Immerse yourself in nature, listen to what nature has to tell you in its quietness so that you can learn and grow.

CHIURA OBATA

French Angelfish, French Grunts, and Smallmouth Grunts

Come forth into the light of things,
let nature be your teacher.

WILLIAM WORDSWORTH

Study nature, love nature, stay close to nature. It will never fail you.

FRANK LLOYD WRIGHT

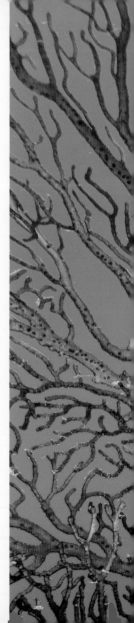

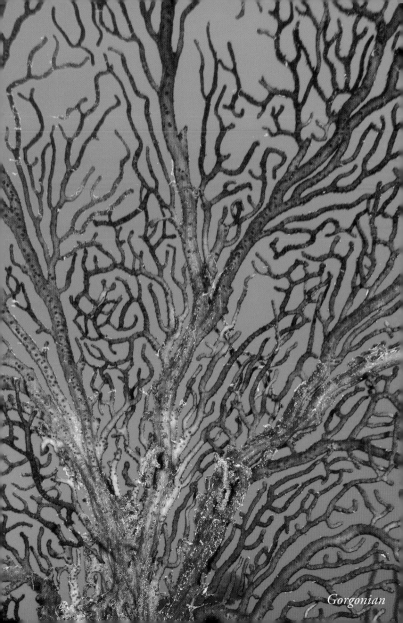

Gorgonian

Giant Hermit Crab Inside Queen Conch Shell

Spider Decorator Crab on Sea Fan

In nature, nothing is
perfect and everything
is perfect.

ALICE WALKER

The sea is everything. It covers seven-tenths of the terrestrial globe. Its breath is pure and healthy. It is an immense desert, where man is never lonely, for he feels life stirring on all sides.

JULES VERNE

Atlantic Spadefish

The good man is the friend of all living things.

MAHATMA GANDHI

Lettuce Leaf Slug

To me the sea is a continual miracle,
The fishes that swim—the rocks—the motion
of the waves—the ships, with men in them.
What stranger miracles are there?

WALT WHITMAN

Queen Triggerfish

Common Bottlenose Dolphin

For whatever we lose
(like a you or a me)
it's always ourselves
we find in the sea.

e.e. cummings

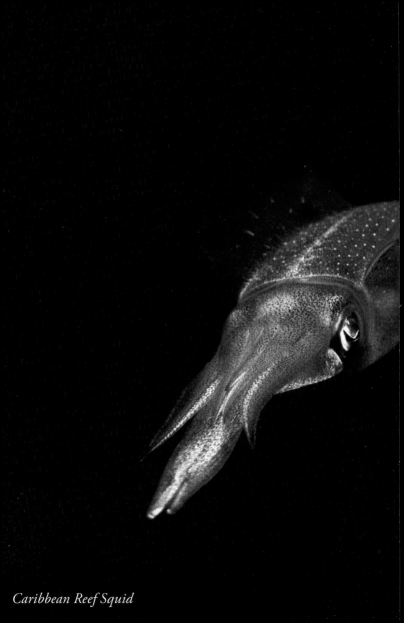

Caribbean Reef Squid

Nature always wears the colors of the spirit.

RALPH WALDO EMERSON

A lot of people attack the sea, I make love to it.

JACQUES-YVES COUSTEAU

I could never stay long enough on the shore; the tang of the untainted, fresh, and free sea air was like a cool, quieting thought.

HELEN KELLER

One touch of nature
makes the whole world
kin.

WILLIAM
SHAKESPEARE

Leatherback Turtle Hatchlings

The sea does not reward those who are too anxious, too greedy, or too impatient. One should lie empty, open, choiceless as a beach—waiting for a gift from the sea.

ANNE MORROW LINDBERGH

Leatherback Turtle Laying Eggs

Hawksbill Turtle Hatchling

Purple Lotus Flower

Wilderness is not a luxury but a necessity of the human spirit.

EDWARD ABBEY

Waterfall at Reef Bay on Petroglyph Spur Trail, St. John

With every drop of water you drink, every breath you take, you're connected to the sea. No matter where on Earth you live.

SYLVIA EARLE

Green-throated Carib Hummingbird

We are tied to the ocean.
And when we go back to the sea, whether
it is to sail or to watch—we are going
back from whence we came.

JOHN F. KENNEDY

To go out with the setting sun
on an empty beach is to truly
embrace your solitude.

JEANNE MOREAU

I love the beach. I love the sea.
All my life I live within—in front of the sea.

RAFAEL NADAL

The cure for anything is salt water:
sweat, tears, or the sea.

ISAK DINESEN

In all things of nature there is something of the marvelous.

ARISTOTLE

We do not associate the idea of antiquity with the ocean, nor wonder how it looked a thousand years ago, as we do of the land, for it was equally wild and unfathomable always.

HENRY DAVID THOREAU

Ruins at Lameshur Bay, St. John

Green is the prime color of the world, and that from which its loveliness arises.

PEDRO CALDERON DE LA BARCA

STEVE SIMONSEN

Steve Simonsen is a world acclaimed photographer with over 26 years of experience and a specialty in underwater photography. His images appear in numerous publications, including *Caribbean Travel and Life*, *Scuba Diving*, and *National Geographic Traveler* magazines. His editorial and advertising photography serves various resorts, airlines, and tourist boards throughout the Caribbean.

Steve's coffee table books include award winning *Living Art*, on St. John; *The United States Virgin Islands*, a photographic portrait; *The British Virgin Islands*, a photographic portrait; and *The Lonely Planet Guide to Diving and Snorkeling in Puerto Rico*. Steve and his wife, Janet, who runs their stock photography business "Marine Scenes," have made St. John their home for the past 23 years.

Friends of **Virgin Islands National Park**

PO Box 811
St. John, VI 00831
www.friendsvinp.org

ISBN: 978-0-692-20560-0
Library of Congress Control Number: 2014939183

Developed, designed, and produced by
Golden Gate National Parks Conservancy,
San Francisco, CA. *www.parksconservancy.org*

DIRECTION: Robert Lieber
DESIGN: Vivian Young, Carol Klammer
EDITOR: Nikki Ahladis
PRODUCTION: Sarah Lau Levitt

Printed in Hong Kong